DISCUSSION PAPER 50

Seven Themes in African Urban Dynamics

Garth Andrew Myers

NORDISKA AFRIKAINSTITUTET, UPPSALA 2010

Indexing terms

Towns
Urbanization
Urban sociology
Literature surveys
Social theory
Urban research

Language checking: Peter Colenbrander

ISSN 1104-8417

ISBN 978-91-7106-677-0

© The author and Nordiska Afrikainstitutet 2010

Print on demand, Lightning Source UK Ltd.

CONTENTS

FOREWORD

The growth of cities is one of the most significant aspects of the contemporary transformation of African societies. Cities in Africa are the sites of major political, economic and social innovation, and thus play a critical role in national politics, domestic economic growth and social development. They are also key platforms for interaction with the wider world and mediate between global and national contexts. Cities are variously positioned in global flows of resources, goods and ideas, and are shaped by varied historical trajectories and local cultures. The result is a great diversity of urban societies across the continent. Cities in Africa are not only growing rapidly but are also undergoing deep political, economic and social transformation. They are changing in ways that defy usual notions of urbanism. In their dazzling complexity, they challenge most theories of the urban. African cities represent major challenges as well as opportunities. Both need to be understood and addressed if a sustainable urban future is to be achieved on the continent. The Urban Cluster of the Nordic Africa Institute, through its research, seeks to contribute to an understanding of processes of urban change in Africa. This discussion paper by Professor Garth Myers, commissioned by the Urban Cluster, is a valuable contribution to shaping the research agenda on urban Africa.

Ilda Lindell
Associate Professor
Leader of the Urban Cluster
The Nordic Africa Institute

INTRODUCTION

As African societies urbanise, it becomes evident that they do so in ways that challenge prevailing theories and models of urban dynamics. This paper surveys the literature of African urban studies to identify key themes for future research. The last ten years have brought a resurgence of interest in urban Africa in the social sciences and humanities. It is thus timely for African studies and urban studies scholars to examine the vibrancy and complexity of African cities with fresh eyes and to learn from African scholarship.

A great range and diversity of contemporary experience exists in the cities of the continent. Recent studies suggest that certain truisms about African cities may be falling by the wayside. The great variation of data on African cities, and variability in their reliability, makes comparison problematic, further challenging the notion that one can still speak of the continent's urban areas as belonging to a single category. The considerable outpouring of urban studies scholarship from Africa is difficult to encompass, since it is considerable and has gone in so many different directions. However, there are certain key literatures and debates that are relatively cross-continental. Thus, scholars are asking how cities deal with:

1. the enduring aftermath of colonialism;
2. the increasing informality of socioeconomic life;
3. urban deprivation, poverty, inequality and sociopolitical exclusion;
4. forms of popular influence, including collective organizing, amid the uncertainties and fluidities in the governance of urban service provision (waste, water, land, housing, electricity and the like) in an era in which neoliberalism both prevails and is contested;
5. warfare, violence and disease;
6. the expanding cosmopolitanism and connectivity of cities; and
7. the imaginative and generative character of urban cultures.

I discuss each theme separately below. In each section, I also suggest ways in which the particular theme might figure in a renewed research agenda on urban Africa. We are seemingly at a point where African urban studies can provide broad, diverse insertions into the discussion of urban theory, and much of what I've written might seem theoretical. Yet the challenges for African urban studies scholarship no longer lie solely in paying more attention to theory only, but also to *practice*, in contributing to efforts to improve the quality of life for urban citizens. This leads me to discuss the policy implications of these themes in my concluding section.

THEME 1
Postcolonial Cities

Perhaps the largest research area in African urban studies over the past 25 years has been the impacts and legacies of colonialism on the continent's cities. Even urban studies or human geography research in Africa that is self-identified as "postcolonial" concentrates on excavating the histories and legacies of colonialism, in part because these were and are so extensive. From this vast literature, certain key themes emerge. The first is the diversity of African experiences of European colonialism, but there remains a strong element of what the historian Catherine Coquery-Vidrovitch (2005a:4) has termed a "shared ... historical rhythm": the most significant investments in the creation of urbanism on African soil coincided with the era of formal colonial rule, roughly from the 1880s to the 1960s. The biggest urban spatial legacy of this "shared rhythm" of European colonialism lies in the location of so many of Africa's major cities along the coast or close to sites of resource extraction, and the functional retardation of African cities into either entrepot/warehouse towns, bureaucratic capitals, or both, rather than as organically grown industrial engines (Freund 2007).

The colonial port-and/or-capital is still a major legacy that has yet to be overcome. Even in 2010, in 46 of the continent's 53 independent states the primary city is the colonial capital, main port or port-capital. Fully 28 of Africa's 50 largest cities are cities of those historical types. The demographic preponderance of the largest of these African urban types has actually increased since 1980, rather than decreased (UN-Habitat 2008). Thirteen of the other 22 largest cities are in Nigeria and South Africa, pointing to another, related element of the colonial legacy. Most African countries other than Nigeria and South Africa have what Western geographers see as poorly developed urban hierarchies, so that very high rates of primacy and the absence of significant secondary cities are still rather common. It is only in the last ten years or so that higher rates of urban population growth have occurred farther down the hierarchy and that growth is slowing in the primary cities (Potts 2009 and 2011). Infrastructural connectivity between cities within countries still lags far behind what the sizes of the cities might suggest, to say nothing of the still weak connectivity between cities in different countries, even where they are near to one another.

In the abstract, high primacy ratios are not immediately disastrous for a country's development. However, what makes the twin challenges of primacy and a thin urban hierarchy more daunting in many African countries is the fact that, with few exceptions, the causes of rapid growth are generally seen as not directly attributable to economic growth and industrialisation (Becker, Hamer, and Morrison 1994; Bryceson 2006). Under colonialism, rural-to-urban migration was fuelled by the pull of perception rather than actual opportunity and by the push factors of rural landlessness, herdlessness, involution, poverty and lack of employment. The end result was that large numbers of rural poor became the urban poor. This conundrum only became more acute in many cities after independence.

Colonialism's other urban legacies relate to internal form and spatial structure. These legacies in African cites are well known and have been widely studied (Celik 1997; Home 1997; Myers 2003; Wright 1991). One legacy is the segregation and segmentation of the urban landscape, while another related legacy is the high degree of inequality, both of which tie into theme 2 below. Often, the most obvious dimension of segmentation in many colonial cities was racial segregation, with separate business and residential areas for Europeans, Asians and Africans, justified rhetorically by concerns about health. Even where white settlement or investment was more limited, as in much of West or Equatorial Africa, this segmentation existed, albeit in modified form (Kawka 2002:42-44). This legacy can be seen in the "distorted" divisions between "high status centers ... and a spreading, sometimes immense, dirt-poor habitat that is poorly served and under-integrated" (Coquery-Vidrovitch 2005a:5).

Colonial cities became laboratories and incubation sites for, and potent physical symbols of, mechanisms of colonial power (Demissie 2007a). In attempting to "replicate a quasi-metropolitan culture in every physical respect," colonial regimes took on the task of normatively reordering African spatiality (Lloyd 2003:107). As centres of power, with growing African populations living in conditions of deprivation, these cities served as crucial arenas for the administrations' drive for order and control expressed in architecture and spatial planning. Urban form expressed ideological concerns spatially (Mitchell 1988; Berman 1984; Myers 2003; Robinson 1990). Colonialism's intertwined strategies seldom worked as intended in any colonial city, but they established patterns and processes that left independent African countries with an apparently daunting legacy to overcome. There is no doubt that colonial regimes established many of the ground rules for urban policy, in terms of building regulations, land administration, housing strategy, spatial organisation and the like (Njoh 2003). Yet quite often, the enforcement of laws or codes or implementation of plans and schemes lagged far behind. The trouble was that ordinary African residents were not empowered to remake or overturn the unenforced and unimplemented ideas. Instead, they simply endured in the interstices between what Europeans wanted from the urban order and what the cities might have been without colonialism.

Yet cities have not made much progress in overcoming the colonial past. Changes to planning laws, building rules, the structures of the world economy, the national urban hierarchy, political processes at urban and national levels, spatial divides and the character of racism are not going to occur overnight, if they are even possible. Still, if African cities have indeed been attempting to subvert or eliminate the colonial legacies over these postcolonial decades, one is fairly often hard-pressed to see the result. In city after city, formerly white or elite areas are increasingly full of gated communities and fortress compounds, while the "dirt-poor habitat" at the other end of the segmented colonial order is even more overcrowded and destitute. Postcolonial regimes have often improved upon the strategies of colonial administrations, becoming even more exclusivist, authoritarian and segmented (Bissell 2007). Thirty years of structural adjustment programmes and poverty reduction strategy papers imposed on African cities by essentially the former colonial powers have meant that "high unemployment, escalating poverty and widening inequality have actually worsened" (Demissie 2007a:7). If postcolonialism is in this sense "something fairly tangible," then it is just as tangibly lacking in being something new, different or better than colonialism for African cities (Yeoh 2001:456).

Postcolonial studies also concentrate on the realms of those promises and uncertainty, beyond tangibles like built environments, and seek to create a "conceptual frame which works to destabilize dominant discourses" (Yeoh 2001:457) and "decolonize the mind" (Ngugi 1986). This reconceptualisation seems to have "promised more than it has delivered" (Driver and Gilbert 1999: 7), at least in terms of reconceiving the state's relationships with people in cities. So if one is looking for postcolonial urban thought in future research, in the sense of thinking that truly attempts to move beyond colonialism, the places to look are probably not government planning offices or posh campuses or the gated compounds of expatriate donors. Instead, it may be found in the "ingenuity with which African urban residents have developed novel strategies" for confronting the "structural and social crisis confronting them" (Demissie 2007a:8). But we must be cautious of blindly championing some sort of post-colonizing of the city from below, given both the potential for non-democratic or repressive city-building that dominates the grassroots and the capacity challenges those grassroots face in taking on re-colonising or neo-colonising states (McEwan 2009).

THEME 2
(I)n(f)ormalising Cities

Informality is as complicated a term as postcolonialism. It may be time to find a new language for this theme, to see it – as my brackets in the heading suggest – as normal and familiar. It has surely generated an extensive and multifaceted literature. Recent writing on the informal sector in urban Africa has argued for "reconsidering" informality more broadly, beyond small business or employment (Hansen and Vaa 2004; Lindell 2010). More economistic conceptualisations miss the wider ways in which housing, land, infrastructure and services, as well as politics and social organisations, develop informally, and the ways in which state agencies, and other formal institutions, act informally – or act to produce informality (Konings, van Dijk, and Foeken 2006; AlSayyad 2004; Roy 2005). It is generally agreed there is a strong trend towards *informalisation* in many African cities, meaning an overall widening of informal activity (Harrison, Todes, and Watson 2008; Grant 2009). The "new waves of informalisation" in the economy typically rely on "forms of work beyond the purview of state regulation or lacking legal protection" and on "casualization and increased precariousness of work" (Lindell 2010:4). These new waves are observable in everyday social lifein the apparently rising importance of unregistered social networks in the built environment, livelihood strategies, social reproduction, cultural organisation or political mobilisation.

My own research interest in this theme lies with the built environment, specifically the growth of informal settlements. Such settlements in urban Africa have a long history. Many African urban areas grew informally from the beginning. Commonly, at least in Atlantic West Africa, such settlements were not considered "squatter settlements" or "slums," in part because the informal rules governing their development were so well understood and enforced via indigenous practices (Konadu-Agyemang 1991:140).

If we conceive of informal settlements as only existing in relation to, and as being the opposite of something we deem to be formal settlements, then clearly European colonialism has again had a significant role in their creation, in the fundamental dichotomy between colonial and colonised zones that ran parallel to distinctions between "modern" and "traditional" economies and cultures (Drakakis-Smith 2000:125). Colonial regimes tended to view informal areas in cities as dangerous and disorderly zones of resistance and detribalisation: no sooner had they begun to emerge than policies were devised that were geared towards their elimination. Those regimes were as often ambivalent, tolerating informal indigenous practices if they benefited the regime. With independence, some national and urban governments attempted to champion the development potential of informal activity, harnessing and thus formalising it. In the last decade, the drive to formalise informal settlements has become almost a religious movement in development circles (Manji 2006).

The capacity to harness informality for formal development goals, and the efficacy of doing so, are questionable. Some elements of informality exist precisely to evade the formal institutions of state and the private sector and profiting from them depends on continued evasion, for example, various forms of corruption or tax and licence avoidance. Because areas of cities dominated by informal arrangements are typically marginalised and poor, it is hardly surprising that planners and urban professionals still abound who are dedicated to the eradication of informality as a way to eliminate poverty. Sometimes eradication is rhetorical, involving adroit recategorisation or a mantra of formalisation. At other times, the push is quite tangible, as in the bulldozing of informal settlements (Harrison, Todes, and Watson 2008:228-33; Kombe and Kreibich 2000).

However, because informal city life is by its very nature "unregistered, unmonitored" and unruly, there is a "severe lack of statistical data" regarding its size, form, function or other characteristics, whether one's aim is to champion it, formalise it or bulldoze it out of existence (Bryceson 2006:9-10). Thus, as difficult as it is to define informality or informal settlements, it is, if anything, more difficult to assess the scope of either. This problem bedevils the recent United Nations Habitat report entitled *The State of African Cities 2008: A Framework for Addressing Urban Challenges in Africa*. Its data on informal sector activity and on what it terms "slum" conditions are both fascinating and problematic. Still, one can reasonably conclude from the report that the scope and proportion of informal settlement and informal sector activity vary across the continent's cities. For this reason, and for its detailed discussion of policy dynamics, the report can be a valuable resource and starting point for analysis of informal settlement.

At the same time, the inexactitude of definition and paucity or inconsistency of data, as well as the apparent pervasiveness of informality within formal ways of doing things in urban Africa, give rise thinking that entirely rejects the language shaping the discussion. "Rather than opposing the 'formal' and the 'informal',," Achille Mbembe and Sarah Nuttall (2008:8) write, "we need a more complex anthropology of things, forms and signs in order to account for the life of the city in Africa." They go on that "the informal is not outside of the formal" and that the "processes of formalization and informalization work together" (Mbembe and Nuttall 2008:9). They argue that research should focus on "how they work together and how this working together ends up producing city forms and urban economies" (Mbembe and Nuttall 2008:9). Though I find their discussion of Johannesburg as "the premier African metropolis, the symbol par excellence of the 'African modern'" (Mbembe and Nuttall 2008:1) extremely problematic (see Robinson 2006, or Murray 2008a), their general conception of informality is a reasonable innovation in the debate. They bring a perspective that questions what many see as "outdated dualities," such as formal vs. informal, and they instead lay stress on urban informality as "an organizing logic" that is gaining prominence in the contemporary era of globalisation and restructuring (AlSayyad 2004:26).

The degree to which the city is angled towards a formal, modernist vision or towards an informal one – or an "Afropolis," as Mbembe and Nuttall (2008:1) call it – varies with each city, as does the geography of the proportioning. The outcomes vary in terms of how formal and informal visions "work together and how this working together" produces space and the space economy of the city. Where there is more clashing than "working together," some ascribe this to "conflicting rationalities" or planning mindsets (Watson 2007:72). Formal planning, "grounded in the rationality of Western modernity and development," holds to one notion of "proper" communities, while the marginalised majority in informal settlements work with a different notion of what a city should be, based on their attempts "to survive, materially and culturally, in … alien places" (Watson 2007:69). In this line of thinking, two deeply and essentially different sets of concepts and practices crash into each other in those cities in urban planning, both in the building and managing of environments through land subdivision and its regulation, housing construction, infrastructure and service provision and the like, and in the attachment of sociocultural meaning and value to such places.

Some scholars don't see these conflicting rationalities as "insurmountable," stressing that the capacity of the urban poor to engage with formal planning processes "is usually limited by the material resources at their disposal rather than 'cultural' factors" (Robins 2006:99). Mbembe and Nuttall, considering the "inherently contradictory, unfinished nature of cities" (Shepherd and Murray 2007:9) and the central role of informal settlements in them, argue for work that can articulate the "virtues of curiosity and astonishment" that emanate from the "practices and imaginations of citiness" in the "other scripts" that lie "beneath the visible landscape" in informal areas (Mbembe and Nuttall 2004:357 and 363; Mbembe and Nuttall 2008). Another, less airy way of getting at their point might be to argue for trying to understand "how urban dwellers in Africa develop their own mechanisms of production and create their own urban forms [and] … developmental norms" (Locatelli and Nugent 2009:7). In most cases, these mechanisms, forms and norms involve a strategic and ever-changing mixture of modernist and non-modernist rationalities, of formal and informal, and future research can develop further understanding of these mechanisms.

The question then becomes whether these other scripts for citiness or mechanisms for producing urban forms and norms, via nimble reframing of harsh reality into survivability, are anything more than that. Is it possible to consciously make and shape informality through alternative channels so that "subaltern reason" can guide planning to "connect with the survival strategies of the poor" (Harrison 2006a:326)? What is the best approach, in practical terms. Should modernist, state-driven planning learn the other scripts and read the city through them? Should the modernist vision be magically made to disappear, allowing the informal ways of planning the Afropolis to essentially be the way the cities grow in its absence? Or should African cities seek some form of "hybrid governance" based on "mutual acceptance" of duelling or interpenetrating rational orders (Trefon 2009:31)? How plausible is such a conceptual drive towards "forging collaborative initiatives between the formal and informal processes" and mindsets (Kombe and Kreibich 2000:148; Myers 2010)?

As with the ideas generated in the attempts to articulate alternative or multiple modernities in relation to Africa (Deutsch, Probst, and Schmidt 2002; Ferguson 2006 and 2008; Geschiere, Meyer, and Pels 2008), the ideas for alternative planning generated from indigenous informality and creativity can be quite inspiring. As Konings, van Dijk and Foeken (2006:3) put it, "the majority of the residents in disadvantaged African neighborhoods have not passively watched conditions deteriorate … they appear to behave as active agents, devising alternative strategies to shape their livelihoods." Yet these alternative strategies may be the small, creative urban practices used by the abject poor to lay claim to "equal rights of membership" in a global urbanity that is both "spectacularly unequal" and highly uneven in its capacity to acknowledge – let alone accept – such claims (Ferguson 2006:175; Ferguson 2008:10; Myers 2010). Informality does insure that "new possibilities emerge, at times in surprising places" (Mbembe and Nuttall 2008:6). Some of these possibilities may be in collective organising in the informal sector, for example (Lindell 2010). But there is still plenty to debate. Some neoliberal theorists and donors champion the informal sector. For others, the whole "crisis of African cities" can be "attributed to the 'informality', 'illegality', and 'anarchy' of their economies" (Locatelli and Nugent 2009:7). Still others see informality as a complex combination of creative and destructive tendencies (Simone 2004). Perhaps the heart of the concerns about what informality means or what to do about informal settlements centres on land issues, literally the foundation of housing issues as well.

Urbanists have long debated the importance of security of tenure. The prevailing argument today within neoliberalism is that residents need secure legal tenure to gain an economic foothold. The neoliberal paradigm almost always includes the drive for security of individuated land tenure. The "greater prominence given to property rights in the development agenda" (Mooya and Cloete 2007:148) is , in part, the result of the wide influence of Hernando de Soto's book, *The Mystery of Capital* (2000), and programmes aimed at land titling for the urban poor (Payne 2002). The key argument of de Soto and others is that formalised and secure property rights reduce poverty. Neoliberals argue that when property rights are poorly or vaguely defined, properties are used wastefully, with high transaction costs, and when they are held in common, they are overexploited (Alston et al. 1996). The urban and periurban poor's best assets are often their properties, the reasoning goes. Therefore, securing their individual control over them allows the poor, cast as "heroic entrepreneurs," to gain the greatest value from them (Alston et al. 1999; Manji 2006). The increased market activity created by lower transaction costs and more secure property rights, if they are achieved through "facilitative institutional arrangements," will, it is claimed, eventually translate into greater economic activity and greater income for the poor (Mooya and Cloete 2007:155). Therefore, the key to bringing to life the "dead capital" of the informal land holdings of the urban poor and raising them from the depths of poverty is the formalisation of property ownership, with government acting merely as a helpmate in land management (de Soto 2000:29; Myers 2008a and 2008b). Relatively uniform land reform laws and programmes have been created across Africa to implement this thesis, despite the fact that the empirical evidence behind de Soto's claims is thin in many settings (Gilbert 2002; Home and Lim 2004; Varley 2002; Myers 2008b; Manji 2006; Ikejiofor 2006).

Within informal systems, increasing numbers of urban residents struggle to access land for building houses (Konings, van Dijk and Foeken 2006:6). As (Lourenço-)Lindell (2002) points out, ordinary residents have very different capacities for exercising informal rights. In many cities, significant tensions arise (or persist) between autochthons and allochthons, or between classes or genders or races (Lindell 2010:16; Konings, van Dyk and Foeken 2006; Grant 2009). Some efforts are made to reach across these divides in organising or deploying informal systems in the interests of the poor majority, but these are still rare (Mitullah 2010).

Cities seem to face the possibility of some kind of Afropolis where informality would essentially be the organising logic, a DeSotoland of formalised informality, or hybrid understandings that more comfortably weave together the already interpenetrating organising logics. Those organising logics are not the same in "informal" cities. Informality and informal settlement also do not have inevitable, predictable, reproducible outcomes in any African city. Easy, one-size-fits-all analyses are inadequate. We might need new terms for the apparently fading dichotomy between formal and informal, given how interwoven they are. Yet these terms are still so much part of shaping the discourse that it is hard to throw them away.

THEME 3
Poor, Unequal and Unjust Cities

Increasing informalisation seems to be a euphemistic way of saying the cities are becoming poorer. They are also becoming more unequal. There does not seem to be one clear way to reduce poverty and inequality, whether by formalising informal areas or processes, allowing the informal systems to take over completely, or working towards hybrid governance, but this latter trend would seem to hold the most emancipatory relational potential. Getting there will mean much more discussion of politics, which takes place below in theme 4.

For theme 3, what first comes to mind about pervasive urban poverty and inequality is the geographical fragmentation and segmentation impacting the psychosocial experience of the city. When the deputy chief of mission in the US embassy invited me in to talk about my research in Lusaka in January 2003, at one point he exclaimed that he had heard that Lusaka really had more than two million people and not the official census population of 1.1 million. "Two million people," he said, "but where are they?" I was too stunned to answer coherently and honestly don't remember now what I said. If I had had my wits about me, I might have said: they are on the move, all around you. Many walk for miles for work, or for the possibility of work. Others are busy farming maize on the little strips between the walls of the estates in your neighbourhood and the streets and other "unimportant, peripheral, and marginal" zones, because they have so little food and so little access to land for farming anywhere else (Simatele and Binns 2008:1). The poor majority of Lusaka, though, had in essence become invisible to this diplomat, as to many elites, including Zambians.

There is again variability in African cities in terms of how pervasive poverty is, or just how unequal these cities are in socio-spatial terms. We again face data problems. Outside South Africa, few African countries have tracked urban data in a manner that enables statistical assessment at the urban scale of poverty and inequality. We can only generalise from a broad array of studies that suggest that urban poverty and deprivation are increasing across most cities, and inequalities widening. For the moment, consider three examples. In Accra, despite great economic strides and the growth of the overall economy, the percentage of the population residing in squalid informal slums has risen in parallel with the proliferation of gated communities with lavish mansions. In Cape Town, despite the tens of millions of euros invested in formal sector housing construction in the Cape Flats through the Reconstruction and Development Programme (RDP) and the Breaking New Ground (BNG) housing programme, even the official percentages of the population residing in "shack settlements" has remained relatively steady, only falling from 19% to 17% over the period of both programmes (and that does not include the subsequent de facto re-informalisation of many houses in RDP/BNG areas). Spectacular homes around the Table Mountain Reserve, meanwhile, sell for tens of millions of rands, often to the glitterati of Hollywood or local tycoons. In Dar es Salaam, even an extraordinary government programme to distribute plots for residential construction met barely one-fifth of existing demand, meaning that even in the best years of managed growth about 80 per cent of housing construction is in increasingly squalid and under-served neighbourhoods, while the elite speculate on beachfront properties on the as-yet undeveloped peninsula across from the downtown, anticipating the billion-shilling investment of a glorious bridge across the harbour.

One could discern this pattern in nearly any African city over the last 20 years. Yet one could also document the increasing capacity among community organisations or non-governmental organisations for combating the growth of poverty and inequality. In many cases, these local activist networks tap into trends towards their empowerment in democratising and decentralising governance structures. To make the new participatory map of governance that dominates urban Africa these days into a relational city, it is, Pieterse (2008a:162) argues, "not enough to have democratic systems and a formal commitment to human rights," but instead "what is required is vigorous democratic contestation." The particular arenas of contestation change with time and geography. There are bound to be fights in any urban society about what it takes to improve the quality of life, or whose quality of life should be improved, or by how much. Research on poverty and inequality is inevitably bound to run into questions of justice. For decades, geographer

David Harvey's (1996:401) work on justice has wrapped itself around the powerful argument that "when encountering a serious problem" such as urban poverty or inequality (whether in terms of distribution or rights), it is "vital ... not merely to try to solve the problem in itself but to confront and transform the processes that gave rise to the problem in the first place." Yet Harvey's (1996:401) concerted call for a "program of radical political action," even as it may ring in the ears, nevertheless suffers from the universalisms of grand theory that make it as problematic as the more conventional liberal thoughts on justice offered by John Rawls (1971). This is particularly so given the maldistribution and injustice visited upon urban African peoples through programmes of "radical political action" on the continent for 40 years or more (Mennasemay 2009).

Encouragingly, some African studies scholars have been turning to the possibilities for an alternative theory of justice built on the ideas of Amartya Sen (1993, 1999). As Maimire Mennesemay (2009:13) has noted, "not much reflection has been devoted" to Sen's ideas as yet in African studies, and the same could be said for much of urban studies. There is far too much to Sen's ideas for me to do them justice here, but his emphases on "the expansion of the 'capabilities' of people to lead the kind of lives they value" (Sen 1999:18) and "the freedom that a person has to lead one kind of life or another" (Nussbaum and Sen 1993:3) are crucial, particularly because Sen makes these capabilities, freedoms and rights *relational*. Although Sen writes about a "person," he is ever cognisant of the social and institutional embeddedness of such persons and this makes his alternative conceptualisation of justice relevant to our questions about urban governance and about poverty or inequality in Africa. "It would be a mistake," Sen (1993:44) argues, to think of a person's "achievements only in terms of active choice by oneself ... There is a very real sense by which the freedom to live the way one would like is enhanced by public policy that transforms epidemiological and social environments." Sen (1993:33) moves the question of social – and environmental – justice out of the realm of distribution, out of the lockdown of individual rights, to more ambiguous realms. He wants to know "how people are enabled" by their society "to imagine, to wonder, to feel emotions such as love and gratitude" (Nussbaum and Sen 1993:1). His language can be vague and ambiguous, and deliberately so, because these questions about such heady matters are complicated and cannot be reduced by numerology to formulas. Sen, a development economist, comes to earth to remind us that "individuals live and operate in a world of institutions. Our opportunities and prospects depend crucially on what institutions exist and how they function" (Sen 1999:142). This last point makes Sen's ideas particularly valuable in understanding justice in African cities.

The thickness and messiness of justice in urban Africa might just be explicable in the following terms: "participation, citizenship and development is not only about inclusion and voice in projects, programs, and policies, but also about politics, power, and influence" (Hendriks 2010:59). Politics, power plays and influences shape the way projects, programmes and policies play out and whether this playing-out improves the quality of life of the poor or ameliorates the socio-environmental injustices in their lives. Julie Crespin's (2006) sensitive critique of the failings of "pro-poor" development assistance comes to mind here. Real reform of governance, she argues, would require "poorer groups having the power and voice to change their relationship with government agencies and other groups at the local level," and yet donors in urban Africa, overwhelmingly, funnel money into "pro-poor" sustainable urban development via government agencies that the vast majority of the urban poor are alienated from and marginalised by (Crespin 2006:434). Crespin (2006:444) argues that "poverty cannot be tackled without addressing problems of power relations and the cultural and social interests that sustain unequal access to economic opportunity and social resources."

Poverty, inequality and injustice are inseparable in African cities, and would be in any governance reforms that would offer solutions to them. Socio-environmental injustice is partly fostered by global processes but ultimately becomes "bound up with … the extent to which low-income groups can influence local government policies" (Nunan and Devas 2004:165). That influence is clearly limited in most African cities, but it varies and it is changing. Future research should follow those changes in the intense, lively and occasionally violent local politics of governance. And it should follow the ways in which politics, power and influence diminish the capacity of the urban poor to effect changes that enhance their capabilities for living lives under improving conditions of their choosing.

THEME 4
Organising, Provisioning and Servicing Cities

There have been a great many efforts at recasting, re-scaling and re-inventing urban governance in Africa, with mixed results. Governance is another very contested and complicated term in African urban studies literature. The word originally meant something like the "manner of governing," but it has come to be linked with decision-making processes that are not limited to the state, "measures that involve setting the rules for the exercise of power and settling conflicts over such rules" (Hyden 1999:185; Hyden et al. 2004; Hendriks 2010; Davies 2008). The last three decades have seen the steady rise of a discourse of "*good* governance" in African cities, ideologically deployed in both the rhetoric and practices of democratisation, privatisation, decentralisation and liberalisation.

The most tangible discussions of good governance in African cities have been in regard to the delivery of *urban services* (sanitation, water, electricity, solid waste, land management and the like). In most African cities through the 1980s, urban service delivery was seen primarily as a responsibility that governments performed, however unevenly or inadequately. Neoliberal advocates of good governance seek privatisation of service delivery and deconcentration of authority away from the state, taking these as given steps towards good governance. Their materialist critics consider every element of neoliberal policy deeply flawed and anti-poor, seldom finding any positive outcomes. A third camp of scholars, which I loosely describe as poststructuralist theorists – when I understand what they are arguing – ask us to think again about the underground, piratic platforms and circulations by which the urban poor survive (Simone 2010). All three camps, ultimately lead us in a set of circles. It is hard to break free of each circle to discern with fresh eyes the complexities of what is occurring on the ground in African cities. The anthropologists Giorgio Blundo and Pierre-Yves Le Meur (2009:2), in introducing their edited volume, *The Governance of Everyday Life in Africa*, aim at analysing the actors involved in actually existing governance, "the way in which the rules for such services are produced, debated, transformed and controlled" and how the urban services themselves are performed in African cities. This seems a fruitful research direction (see also Fredericks (2009) on solid waste management in Dakar). Both Fredericks and the Blundo/Le Meur book would concur with geographer Anna Davies's (2008:25) observation that debates on governance in urban studies, political science and urban geography remain long on conceptualisation and abstraction.

That gives rise to a growing advocacy for more grounded, empirical assessments. In Africa, it seems increasingly evident that both the directions and outcomes of shifts from government to governance do vary, particularly in the sphere of service delivery

(McDonald 2009; McCarney and Stren 2003). In moving towards empirical assessment of this variation, Pieterse (2008a:162) suggests that we need to pay particular attention to the "systemic drivers of urban development." These drivers include the way decision-making processes work in local urban politics, how infrastructure is built, technology deployed and landscapes shaped in creating and re-creating a city's spatial structure, and both how economic activity works and how local structures and agents work to address the inequalities that result.

We are in an era when the dominant voices of donors, the state and local elites sing the praises of more participatory, democratic governance and decision-making in urban service delivery. Materialist and poststructuralist critics, in different ways, see the ethos of this era as fatally flawed. More empirical analyses on the ground, with a focus on service delivery outcomes, also seem critical, while at the same time offering a cautious openness towards a new political era in African cities.

THEME 5

Wounded Cities

For some cities, it is a stretch to even contemplate a new political era, or even empirical analysis on the ground. Urbicide is part of the story of African cities, where open warfare and persistent violent conflict have made rubble of the cityscape, or HIV/AIDS and other pandemic or endemic diseases threaten so many lives in cities north, south, east or west on the map of Africa. There is a "continuum" to definitions of urban violence in Africa that is worth articulating at the outset (Scheper-Hughes and Bourgeois, in Ahluwalia et al. 2007:1). One must be wary of romancing the "pervasive, almost ritualistic, association of Africa with forms of everyday as well as extreme violence" (Ahluwalia et al. 2007:1). At one end of the continuum, it is important to note the degree to which many cities on the continent can be characterised by the *non-violence* operating alongside forms of violence (Simone 2007; Schler 2007). Then there are many other cities where there is no outright war but a considerable amount of mundane violence: the example comes to mind of Maiduguri, Nigeria in July 2009, when five days of street violence erupted in a rather quiet and conservative city. AbdouMaliq Simone (2006) recently posited a conception of piracy as a form of governance and explored its applicability to cities such as Douala, Johannesburg, Lagos or Kinshasa. Certainly this is piracy not lacking in violence and wounds, and these are longer, slower and deeper episodes than those of Maiduguri. Kinshasa, in Theodore Trefon's (2009:3) words, is "portrayed as a forsaken black hole characterized by calamity, chaos, confusion and … social cannibalism where society is its own prey."

There is a more than perceptible difference between ill-governed cities subsisting under shadows of crime and social despair, yet where "new and remarkable patterns of stability, organization and quest for well-being have emerged" (Trefon 2009:3) and cities that endure year after year of open and outright urban civil warfare. Jean Omasombo (2005:96) has written of Kisangani, Congo, as a "city at its lowest ebb" in the early 2000s, following its destruction in the civil war that followed the DRC's independence in 1960 and the "heavy toll" it paid in "the protracted war that began in 1998" and has not yet really ended. Omasombo (2005:99) demonstrates that Kisangani "stands as the symbol of the collapse of the whole of Congo," and its residents have little capacity for the "resourcefulness displayed in other towns," because it is so centrally situated in violent war.

I am not well qualified to strategise on health policies, policing, international relations or even general security issues. Yet it is hard to contemplate improving urban dynamics in Africa without the peaceful resolution of conflict and the reduction of violence, in some settings of violent crime. Likewise, one can plan and build the most efficient and effective new city, but it becomes harder and harder to sustain the efficiency and effectiveness if a third of the population is chronically ill with a potentially life-threatening disease. As a geographer, my approach is to think about urban space in relation to these questions about wounds, whether from violence or disease. David Harvey (2000:182), in *Spaces of Hope*, asks us to think about creating "possibilities of spatial form" that might foster "a wide range of human potentialities." Geographer Patricia Daley (2007:235) responds to Harvey at the very end of her book, *Gender and Genocide in Burundi*, that "finding spaces of hope [will] require actual engagement with emancipatory politics" and the "rehumanization of African people." One way that must happen is by decentring discussion of urban experience to be able to encompass and re-hear what people in peripheral informal settlements are saying about their cities.

In my forthcoming book, I analyse Nuruddin Farah's most recent fiction for its possibilities for an African urban theory in which even the most wounded cities – in this case Mogadishu – might contribute to alternative modes of seeing urbanism. My reasoning is that it is sometimes among the artists, writers and dreamers that the best new visions arise. Farah belongs to an emerging cadre of postcolonial African novelists creating what John Marx (2008:597) calls "failed state fiction." This is a genre that seeks to "shape a counterdiscourse" to the social science conception of a failed state (Marx 2008:599). Farah, like other novelists originating in failed states, uses his fiction in part to "present competent management as an aspiration every bit as compelling as the goal of national liberation it displaces" in earlier post-independence African novels (Marx 2008:597). What Peter Hitchcock (2007:745) considers Farah's "wild imaginings" in his novels offer not just escape from what Hitchcock calls "brute materiality": they are also part of domesticating alternatives to the postcolonial reality. It is regularly in remaking a house, in reconstructing a family, or in rebuilding trust in friendships that Farah situates Mogadishu's rebirth and its process of healing its wounds.

Through Farah's eyes, we see the city again, never without its fractures, grief, absurdity or misery, but also never without hope. A Farah novel "*does* something, rather than just means something," as R. John Williams (2006:163) would have it, because "its imaginative interventions into historiography dramatize the potential to shape reality." Through consideration of Farah's recreation of Mogadishu as a lived space, in Henri Lefebvre's (1991) sense of it, Farah breathes life back into the city. Imaginary space is no substitute for practical, activist work towards conflict resolution, to which Farah quietly devotes a considerable amount of energy, outside the novels (Farah 2007b). But it is also in the antinationalist, global connectivity Farah foregrounds that his novels relink Mogadishu as a city in a world of cities (Ngaboh-Smart 2000, 2001, 2004). Like other African literary "escapees from the destructive authoritarianisms of postcolonial rule," Farah is "caught up in the maelstrom of massive international migrations," seeking to articulate the connections between these two phenomena (Zeleza 2005:11). In his novels, Farah is doing something quite different from his oft-repeated desire to keep "his country alive by writing about it": he is deterritorialising Somalia as a nationalist project and reterritorialising it as a place that belongs in the world, with its capital city at the heart of that belonging by "straddling" (Ngaboh-Smart 2001:97; Gikandi 2002).

In Farah's vision, Mogadishu is no longer the "world-capital-of-things-gone-to-hell," whose people get what's coming to them. My point is that in looking at cities like Mogadishu, it is less a question of policy: there can be no real rebirth for Mogadishu without imagination. Lefebvre (1991:378-79 and 400) reminds us that perceived, conceived and lived spatiality still "meet at the crossroads"; that "the proliferation of links and networks, by directly connecting up very diverse places ... tends to render the state redundant"; and that "innumerable groups" seek "to invent new forms." Although, "an architecture of pleasure and joy, of community in the use of the gifts of the earth, has yet to be invented" (Lefebvre, 1991:379), these liberated, lived spaces provide vital counter-spaces to the perceived and conceived spaces of the dominant elites and for reflecting on the impacts of disease, violence and warfare on African cities.

THEME 6
Cosmopolitan Cities

The philosopher Kwame Anthony Appiah (2006:xiv) takes us back to the roots of the term "cosmopolitan" in 4th century BCE Cynicism: "citizen of the cosmos," where a citizen "belonged to a particular city" and at the same time to "the world ... in the sense of the universe." He argues for cosmopolitanism not as the answer to the world's problems, but as a challenge, "a gauntlet thrown down." There are many cities in Africa and a great many people in them that can and should be conceived as cosmopolitan – indeed, have been for many centuries – and there is a growing literature on Africa's cities that discusses cosmopolitanism. Cosmopolitanism, like my other theme-words, is a very complicated term with ever-shifting definitional values (Nava 2007). Soja (2000:229-32) used the term "cosmopolis" as one of his six discourses on the postmetropolis, borrowing from a number of scholars who had also used this term, such as Stephen Toulmin, Engin Isin and Leonie Sandercock. His discussion of their work suggests, as Appiah's idea of cosmopolitanism does, a helpful means of seeing both the very deep histories of interplay between cities and globalisation and the ways in which contemporary globalisation is not simply a negative force, but also a "source of new opportunities and challenges" (Soja 2000:231). Mica Nava (2007:3) adds to this the notion by seeing cosmopolitanism as – in Raymond Williams's sense – a "structure of feeling" or "an empathetic and inclusive set of identifications" that people belonging to or identifying with a particular city have with one another and with worldly ideas.

One of the deepest expressions of cosmopolitanism in Africa is Zanzibar, where I've done a lot of my own research and where "intense global interconnectivity" was a defining feature of city life from the 18th century CE onward. Indeed, the Swahili coast exists as a culture region because of this interconnectivity from the 1st century BCE, picking up in intensity in the medieval period (Prestholdt 2008:89; Genscheimer 2004; Sheriff 1987; Larsen 2009). Contemporary globalisation has done nothing but further the worldliness of the connections and even when boxed in by a colonial or socialist order it produces new opportunities along with challenges (Bang 2008).

In considering how globalisation and cosmopolitanism impact African urban dynamics, many scholars deploy conceptualisations of diasporas and transnationality. Sheffer (1986:3) defined *diaspora* as a minority ethnic group "of migrant origins residing and acting in host countries but maintaining strong sentimental and material links with their countries of origin." Africanist geographers are increasingly interested in the links of diaspora communities back into the politics and development programmes of countries of origin, or around the world (Mercer, Page and Evans 2008). Migration patterns become less unidirectional, as the "broad topography of interconnections" (Simone 2004:119) of African communities expands. Great hopes for development are placed on new African diaspora communities. The UK's Department for International Development, for one, "sees in recent African diasporas the opportunity for the African continent to benefit from globalization ... [and] reverse the deleterious effects of the 'brain drain'" (Koser 2003:10). It is, however, uncertain how significant a force for African development diaspora communities can be. There are great differences "both between and within" African diasporas, with some demonstrating reasons for the hope that DFID and others have placed in them, and others dominated by internal fractures, illegality, exclusivity or elitism (Koser 2003:10).

Transnationality can be defined as the status of people who are "at least bi-lingual, move easily between different cultures, frequently maintain homes in two countries, and pursue economic, political, and cultural interests that require simultaneous presence in both" (Portes 1997:16). Gupta and Ferguson (1992: 9) see transnationality as a kind of "bifocal" experience – where migrants think both locally and globally, with varying degrees of success. Gilroy's (1995:26; 1993) arguably more poetic way of meshing the "roots and routes" comes in the form of his notion of the "changing same" in African diasporas, where ideas of what-and-where a people have been, are and are becoming actually share space and time. The "changing same" idea is appealing, but it is a notion that depends on forging collective memory, and in practice this can be difficult to separate from the homogenizing power dynamics of nationalism or class (K. Mitchell 2005).

Many new African diaspora community members live a less well-financed version of the "new cosmopolitanism" spoken of by Appiah (2006:32), involving people with "many intimate connections with places far away." This leads them towards increasing participation in local cultural institutions, but also to deeper commitments around the globe, especially, though not exclusively, in their countries of origin. Transnationality can produce what Appiah terms a healthy "contamination" of cultures. Transnational spaces are always in motion and collision. Yet the concept also implies less positive contamination, "a kind of passage, yet a passage that encompasses the possibility of never arriving. Of drifting endless on the betwixt and between of the world's boundaries ... of being 'other' among the established" (Carter 2003:xiv; Carter 2010). This endless drift and contamination leaves many African transnationals living in a "disaffected space of inauthentic citizenship," forced to form "nomadic identities" out of the "trauma of dispossession and displacement" (Joseph 1999:3). Development planning needs to reconsider and problematise the degree to which ideas of hybridity, ambivalence or rhizome networks in postcolonial studies of African diasporas can be deployed in political projects of democratisation or community building. Although there is "undeniable appeal" in the "critical possibilities" of diaspora discourse, these political projects also include "reifications of their own" (Dirlik 2001:85).

THEME 7
Imaginative Cities

Much of what happens in African cities is invisible, unpredictable and apparently bizarre to the unfamiliar visitor. Sometimes, this invisibility is inexplicable, and sometimes it seems deliberate. The widely available roadmap to Lusaka, for example, has advertisements scattered all around its edges. They cover up the vast majority of Lusaka's "peri-urban areas," where two-thirds of the city's population resides (Waste Management Unit 2006). Many of the names of these compounds do appear on the map, but none of the roads that cut across and through them do. One could never use the map to navigate them: these "unauthorised" areas are largely invisible to the map's users. This circumstance symbolises an invisibility that haunts a great many African cities. Yet in and around this invisibility, incredibly imaginary and imaginative facets of the city emerge, creative, propulsive, innovative and strongly linked with a wider world.

"Our imaginations have lived so long with the ... deadening images of power drawn on the ground ... Can we begin to shift our experiences and our visions to capture the world of always-moving spaces? What do the spaces of dynamism and change look like?" The geographer Jennifer Robinson (1998:D5) asked these questions in the early post-apartheid days in South Africa. In the dozen years since her piece was published, across the continent, with increasing frequency, collaborative and creative energies of different cities reach across borders into "always-moving spaces." Although Robinson was writing directly about apartheid South African cities, her passage opens out on to a more continental moment of a multiplicity of attempts to shift experiences and visions in imaginations, from Johannesburg detective stories to Nollywood videos from Lagos (Nuttall 2008:215; Barrot 2008). The globalizing and stretching of citiness brings urban Africa into links, whether informal, unruly and wounded, with other cities around the world. A move towards critical analysis of African urban cultures *in situ* and in connectivities with processes of globalisation is abundantly evident in African urban studies in general.

For example, international arts festivals, whether focused on music, film, theatre, dance, sculpture, photography or painting, or all of the above, are crucial sites of worlding, often for smaller cities. Grahamstown hosts South Africa's National Arts Festival. St. Louis, Senegal, a town of a similar size, history and educational focus, has hosted the St. Louis jazz festival, arguably Africa's most significant international jazz festival. Like Grahamstown, St. Louis has also built itself into an international tourist destination with a combination of a festival and a dedication to highlighting its bloody history – in this case, as a UNESCO World Heritage site. Ouagadougou, Burkina Faso has ridden a similar globalizing wave via FESPACO, the Pan-African Film and Television Festival of Ouagadougou, which has grown since its 1969 founding into Africa's largest and most globally significant such festival. Essaouira, Morocco, a UN Localizing Agenda 21 showcase city, has hosted the Gnaoua (Gnawa) and World Music Festival, meshing ecstatic Sufi spiritual performance with an increasingly wide array of world music forms and attracting an ever increasing international audience (Kapchan 2008). Not to be outdone, Zanzibar holds both an international film festival (ZIFF, or the Festival of the Dhow Countries) and an international music festival. Similar globally marketed international arts festivals occur in Cape Town, Essakane and Segou, Mali, Casablanca, Rabat, Carthage, Harare and elsewhere. It would be easy to dismiss many of these as copycats, thin or shallow expressions of deep local cultures, disorganised messes, or borderline financial successes. But taken as a whole, the festivalisation of African cities, even for a few days a year in each case, marks the profoundly cosmopolitan, globalised, imaginative, generative and dynamic character of the continent's "always-moving spaces."

Visual artists – photographers, painters and sculptors alike – are also directly re-envisioning urban Africa without collaborations with academic urbanists. The artist Julie Mehretu has developed a very geographical body of work that visualises alternative modes of seeing cities. Novelists, artists and the ordinary people in cities and in exile from them are the sources of alternative visions of theory and practice for African urbanism. But there are plenty of professional place-makers among African urban planners and architects seeking to develop and implement imaginative alternative urban visions. A new generation of African architects and planners, for example, is busily engaged in re-envisioning the continent's cities. The first order of business for some of these practising architects and planners is tracing – writing and in some cases rewriting – the varied and deep histories of architecture and urban planning on the continent (Elleh 1997 and 2002). Others have experimented with possibilities for developing an Afrocentric architecture out of that history (Hughes 1994). Still more are engaged in re-envisioning the training processes in architecture and planning schools on the continent to incorporate African processes of planning and sociocultural influences on building and urban design. This has in turn led to collective and collaborative research that enables African architects and planners to both compare what is happening in one another's cities and to work towards non-Eurocentric visions of cities. It is vital to incorporate some of that new thinking about urban space into future urban research.

CONCLUSION
Policy Directions

Once we've contemplated these seven themes, the goals for producing work with "practical usefulness in changing the world for the better" Soja (2000) become a mouthful: *to improve the quality of life for all, while including more and different people in democratic decision-making within an overall framework that works towards an expansion of social and environmental justice through a thick and messy realignment of state-society relations that enhance people's capabilities for leading the lives they choose*. The path there will not be universal for African cities: it will always be contested and it will always take a different shape in different cities and different times. Keeping in mind my seven themes above, let me close this "state-of-the-art" paper with seven priority areas for urban research, as follows:

(1) Continued engagement with research on colonial legacies, but tied into means for overcoming these, whether in rewriting colonial-era building rules or investing in infrastructure for underdeveloped areas in the urban hierarchy.

(2) Baseline research and data creation for assessing informalisation and how informal and formal sectors and settlements work together or go together in cities across the continent, particularly in the spheres of labour and housing, in collective organising and in the built environment.

(3) Related research on hybrid forms of governance between informal and formal, particularly in the realm of service provision, which can move the debate past its neoliberalism-good-vs.-neoliberalism-bad impasse, but minus the potentially alienating language of some works influenced by poststructuralist thought.

(4) Research to critically analyse democratisation in urban dimensions, in terms of provisioning, poverty alleviation, amelioration of inequalities and socio-environmental justice.

(5) Critical analysis of security issues, conflict resolution processes, crime and policing and health crises as they impact African cities, remaining open to emancipatory creative thinking and re-visions.

(6) Empirical assessment of the links between African cities and diaspora communities abroad in terms of how transnational organisations do, or do not, transform urban development processes on the continent.

(7) Learning from African artists, writers, architects and planners as they seek new visions of the continent's cities.

Inevitably, my seven priorities are bound to be different from those others might choose, or my phraseology may be different from another scholar's approach. It is therefore important to be open to a wide range of methodological approaches – from literary criticism or archival analysis to statistical surveys and geographical information systems science. The terrain is quite wide open and we need an ecumenical appreciation of the tools in the toolkit. One major gap, in fact, is evident in the continuing dearth of data collected under comparable conditions. The African Centre for Cities at the University of Cape Town, in conjunction with the World Bank Cities Alliance and various local offices of Slum Dwellers International, seeks to overcome this with its ambitious programme for the creation of State of the Cities reports for more than 30 cities on the continent, but the project has a long way to go. But it is important to engage in critical research, using a wide range of methods in a diverse array of urban contexts, that can inform policy and future development planning in new and more sustainable directions.

REFERENCES

Ahluwalia, P., L. Bethlehem and R. Ginio (eds) (2007), *Violence and Non-Violence in Africa*, Routledge, New York.

AlSayyad, N. (2004), 'Urban Informality as a "New" Way of Life', in A. Roy and N. AlSayyad (eds.), *Urban Informality: Transnational Perspectives from the Middle East, Latin America, and South Asia*, Lexington Books, Lanham, MD, pp. 7-30.

Alston, L., T. Eggertsson, and D. North (1996), *Empirical Studies in Institutional Change*, Cambridge University Press, Cambridge.

Alston, L., G. Libecap, and B. Mueller (1999), *Titles, Conflict and Land Use: The Development of Property Rights on the Brazilian Frontier*, University of Michigan Press, Ann Arbor.

Appiah, K. (2006), *Cosmopolitanism: Ethics in a World of Strangers*, Norton, New York.

Bang, A. (2008), 'Cosmopolitanism Colonised? Three Cases from Zanzibar 1890-1920', in E. Simpson and K. Kresse (eds.), *Struggling with History: Islam and Cosmopolitanism in the Western Indian Ocean*, Columbia University Press, New York, pp. 167-188.

Barrot, P. (ed.) (2008), *Nollywood: The Video Phenomenon in Nigeria*, James Currey, Oxford.

Becker, C., A. Hamer, and A. Morrison (1994), *Beyond Urban Bias in Africa: Urbanization in an Era of Structural Adjustment*, Heinemann, Portsmouth, New Hampshire.

Berman, B. (1984), 'Structure and Process in the Bureaucratic States of Colonial Africa', *Development and Change*, vol. 15, no. 1, pp. 23-41.

Bissell, W. (2007), 'Casting a Long Shadow: Colonial Categories, Cultural Identities, and Cosmopolitan Spaces in Globalizing Africa', in F. Demissie (ed.), *Postcolonial African Cities: Imperial Legacies and Postcolonial Predicaments*, Routledge, New York, pp. 25-41.

Blundo, G., and P-Y. Le Meur (2009), 'Introduction: an Anthropology of Everyday Governance: Collective Service Delivery and Subject-Making', in G. Blundo and P-Y. Le Meur (eds.), *The Governance of Daily Life in Africa: Ethnographic Explorations of Public and Collective Services*, Brill, Leiden, pp. 1-37.

Bryceson, D. (2006), 'Fragile Cities: Fundamentals of Urban Life in East and Southern Africa', in D. Bryceson and D. Potts (eds.), *African Urban Economies: Viability, Vitality or Vitiation?* Palgrave Macmillan, New York, pp. 3-38.

Carter, D. (2003), 'Preface', in K. Koser (ed.), *New African Diasporas*, Routledge, London, pp. ix-xix.

Carter, D. (2010), *Navigating the African Diaspora*, University of Minnesota Press, Minneapolis.

Celik, Z. (1997), *Urban Forms and Colonial Confrontations: Algiers under French Rule*, University of California Press, Berkeley.

Coquery-Vidrovitch, C. (2005a), *The History of African Cities South of the Sahara from the Origins to Colonization*, Markus Weiner, Princeton.

Coquery-Vidrovitch, C. (2005b), 'Urban Cultures: Relevance and Context', in T. Falola and S. Salm (eds.), *Urbanization and African Cultures*, Carolina Academic Press, Durham, NC, pp. 17-22.

Crespin, J. (2006), 'Aiding Local Action: the Constraints Faced by Donor Agencies in Supporting Effective, Pro-Poor Initiatives on the Ground', *Environment and Urbanization,* vol. 18, no. 4, pp. 433-449.

Daley, P. (2007), *Gender and Genocide in Burundi: The Search for Spaces of Peace in the Great Lakes Region*, James Currey, Oxford.

Davies, A. (2008), *The Geographies of Garbage Governance: Interventions, Interactions and Outcomes*, Ashgate, Aldershot.

De Soto, H. (2000), *The Mystery of Capital: Why Capitalism Triumphs in the West and Fails Everywhere Else*, Basic Books, New York.

Demissie, F. (2007a), 'Imperial Legacies and Postcolonial Predicaments: an Introduction', in
    F. Demissie (ed.), *Postcolonial African Cities: Imperial Legacies and Postcolonial Predicaments*,
    Routledge, New York, pp. 1-10.

Demissie, F. (2007b), 'Visual Fragments of Kinshasa', in F. Demissie (ed.), *Postcolonial African
    Cities: Imperial Legacies and Postcolonial Predicaments*, Routledge, New York, pp. 131-142.

Deutsch, J-G., P. Probst, and H. Schmidt (eds.) (2002), *African Modernities: Entangled Meanings in
    Current Debate*, James Currey, Oxford.

Dirlik, A. (2001), 'Place-Based Imagination: Globalism and the Politics of Place', in R. Prazniak
    and A. Dirlik (eds.), *Places and Politics in an Age of Globalization*, Rowman & Littlefield,
    Lanham, MD, pp. 15-51.

Drakakis-Smith, D. (2000), *Third World Cities*, 2nd edition, Routledge, London.

Driver, F., and D. Gilbert (1999), 'Imperial Cities: Overlapping Territories, Intertwined Histories',
    in F. Driver and D. Gilbert (eds.), *Imperial Cities: Landscape, Display and Identity*, Manchester University Press, Manchester, pp. 1-17.

Elleh, N. (1997), *African Architecture: Evolution and Transformation*, McGraw-Hill, New York.

Elleh, N. (2002), *Architecture and Power in Africa*, Praeger, New York.

Farah, N. (2007a), *Knots*, Riverhead (Penguin) Books, New York:.

Farah, N. (2007b), 'My Life as a diplomat', *The New York Times*, 26 May.

Ferguson, J. (2006), *Global Shadows: Africa in the Neoliberal World Order*, Duke University Press,
    Durham, NC.

Ferguson, J., (2008), 'Global Disconnect: Abjection and the Aftermath of Modernism', in
    P. Geschiere, B. Meyer, and P. Pels (eds.), *Readings in Modernity in Africa,* Indiana University Press, Bloomington, IN, pp. 8-16.

Fredericks, R. (2009), 'Doing the Dirty Work: The Cultural Politics of Garbage Collection in
    Dakar, Senegal', unpublished PhD thesis, University of California, Berkeley.

Freund, B. (2007), *The African City*, Cambridge University Press, Cambridge.

Gensheimer, T. (2004), 'Globalization and the Medieval Swahili City', in T. Falola and S. Salm,
    (eds.), *Globalization and Urbanization in Africa*, Africa World Press, Trenton, NJ,
    pp. 171-185.

Geschiere, P., B. Meyer, and P. Pels (2008), 'Introduction', in P. Geschiere, B. Meyer, and P. Pels
    (eds.), *Readings in Modernity in Africa*, Indiana University Press, Bloomington, pp. 1-7.

Gikandi, S. (2002), 'The Politics and Poetics of National Formation: Recent African Writing and
    Maps', in D. Wright (ed.), *Emerging Perspectives on Nuruddin Farah*, Africa World Press,
    Trenton, NJ, pp. 449-468.

Gilbert, A. (2002), 'On the Mystery of Capital and the Myths of Hernando de Soto: What Difference Does Legal Title Make?', *International Development Planning Review*, vol. 24, no. 1,
    pp. 1-19.

Gilroy, P. (1993), *The Black Atlantic: Modernity and Double Consciousness*, Verso, London.

Gilroy, P. (1995), 'Roots and Routes: Black Identity as an Outernational Project', in H. Harris,
    H. Blue, and E. Griffith (eds.), *Racial and Ethnic Identity: Psychological Development and
    Creative Expression*, Routledge, London, pp. 15-30.

Grant, R. (2009), *Globalizing City: The Urban and Economic Transformation of Accra, Ghana,* Syracuse University Press, Syracuse.

Gupta, A., and J. Ferguson (1992), 'Beyond "Culture": Space, Identity, and the Politics of Difference', *Cultural Anthropology,* vol. 7, pp. 6-23.

Hansen, K., and M. Vaa (eds.) (2004), *Reconsidering Informality: Perspectives from Urban Africa*,
    Nordic Africa Institute Press, Uppsala.

Harrison, P. (2006a), 'On the Edge of Reason: Planning and Urban Futures in Africa', *Urban Studies,* vol. 43, no. 2, pp. 319-335.

Harrison, P. (2006b), 'Integrated Development Plans and Third Way Politics', in U. Pillay, R. Tomlinson, and J. du Toit (eds.), *Democracy and Delivery: Urban Policy in South Africa*, HSRC Press, Pretoria.

Harrison, P., A. Todes, and V. Watson (2008), *Planning and Transformation: Learning from the Post-Apartheid Experience*, Routledge, New York.

Harvey, D. (2000), *Spaces of Hope*, Edinburgh University Press, Edinburgh.

Harvey, D. (1996), *Justice, Nature, and the Geography of Difference*. Blackwell, Oxford.

Hendriks, B. (2010), 'City-Wide Governance Networks in Nairobi: Towards Contributions to Political Rights, Influence and Service Delivery for Poor and Middle-Class Citizens?', *Habitat International*, vol. 34, no. 1, pp. 59-77.

Hitchcock, P. (2007), 'Postcolonial Failure and the Politics of Nation', *South Atlantic Quarterly*, vol. 106, no. 4, pp. 727-752.

Home, R. (1997), *Of Planting and Planning: The Making of British Colonial Cities*, Spon, London.

Home, R., and H. Lim (2004), *Demystifying the Mystery of Capital: Land Tenure and Poverty in Africa and the Caribbean*, Glasshouse Press, London.

Hughes, D. (1994), *Afrocentric Architecture: a Design Primer*, Greydon Press, Dayton, OH.

Hyden, G. (1999), 'Governance and the Reconstitution of Political Order', in R. Joseph (ed.), *State, Conflict and Democracy in Africa*, Lynne Rienner, Boulder, pp. 179-96.

Hyden, G., J. Court, and K. Mease (2004), *Making Sense of Governance: Empirical Evidence from Sixteen Developing Countries*, Lynne Rienner, Boulder.

Ikejiofor, U. (2006), 'Equity in Informal Land Delivery: Insights from Enugu, Nigeria', *Land Use Policy*, vol. 23, pp. 448-59.

Joseph, M. (1999), *Nomadic Identities: The Performance of Citizenship*, University of Minnesota Press, Minneapolis.

Kapchan, D. (2008), 'Performing the Festive Sacred in Morocco: Sufi Tourism and the Promise of Sonic Translation', paper presented to the Kansas African Studies Center Seminar Series, 21 April.

Kawka, R. (2002), 'The Physiognomic Structure of Maiduguri', in R. Kawka (ed.), *From Bulamari to Yerwa to Metropolitan Maiduguri: Interdisciplinary Studies on the Capital of Borno State, Nigeria*, Rödiger Köppe Verlag, Köln, pp. 33-63.

Kombe, W., and Kreibich, V. (2000), *Informal Land Management in Tanzania*, SPRING Research Series 29, University of Dortmund, Dortmund, Germany.

Konadu-Agyemang, K. (1991), 'Reflections on the Absence of Squatter Settlements in West Africa', *Urban Studies*, vol. 28, pp. 139-151.

Konings, P., R. van Dijk and D. Foeken (2006), 'The African Neighborhood: an Introduction, in P. Konings and D. Foeken (eds.), *Crisis and Creativity: Exploring the Wealth of the African Neighborhood*, Brill, Leiden, pp. 1-21.

Koser, K. (2003), 'New African Diasporas: an Introduction', in K. Koser (ed.), *New African Diasporas*, Routledge, London, pp. 1-16.

Larsen, K. (2009), 'Introduction', in K. Larsen (ed.), *Knowledge, Ritual and Religion: Repositioning and Changing Ideological and Material Circumstances among the Swahili on the East African Coast*, Nordic Africa Institute Press, Uppsala, pp. 11-37.

Lefebvre, H. (1991), *The Production of Space*, Blackwell, Oxford.

Lindell, I. (2010), 'Changing Landscapes of Collective Organizing in the Informal Economy', in I. Lindell (ed.), *Africa's Informal Workers: Collective Agency, Alliances, and Transnational Organizing*, Nordic Africa Institute Press, Uppsala, pp. 4-34.

Lloyd, R. (2003), 'Defining Spatial Concepts toward an African Urban System', *Urban Design International*, vol. 8, pp. 105-117.

Locatelli, F., and P. Nugent (2009), 'Introduction', in F. Locatelli and P. Nugent (eds.), *African Cities: Competing Claims on Urban Spaces*, Leiden, Brill, pp. 1-13.

Lourenço-Lindell, I. (2002), *Walking the Tight Rope: Informal Livelihoods and Social Networks in a West African City*, Stockholm University Press, Stockholm.

Manji, A. (2006), *The Politics of Land Reform in Africa: From Communal Tenure to Free Markets*, Zed Books, London.

Marx, J. (2008), 'Failed State Fiction', *Contemporary Literature*, vol. 49, no. 4, pp. 597-633.

Mbembe, A., and S. Nuttall (2008), 'Introduction: Afropolis', in S. Nuttall and A. Mbembe (eds.), *Johannesburg: The Elusive Metropolis*, Duke University Press, Durham, NC, pp. 1-33.

Mbembe, A., and S. Nuttall (2004), 'Writing the World from an African Metropolis', *Public Culture*, vol. 16, no. 2.

McCarney, P. and R. Stren (eds.) (2003), *Governance on the Ground: Innovations and Discontinuities in Cities of the Developing World*, Woodrow Wilson Center Press, Washington, DC.

McDonald, D. (2009), 'Electric Capitalism: Conceptualising Electricity and Capital Accumulation in (South) Africa', in D. McDonald (ed.), *Electric Capitalism: Recolonising Africa on the Power Grid*, Earthscan, London, pp. 1-49.

McEwan, C. (2009), *Postcolonialism and Development*, Routledge, New York.

Mennasemay, M. (2009), 'A Millennium Development Goal for Ethiopia: Some Conceptual Issues', *Africa Today*, vol. 55, no. 1, pp. 3-32.

Mercer, C., B. Page, and M. Evans (2008) *Development and the African Diaspora: Place and the Politics of Home*, Zed Books, London.

Mitchell, K. (2005), 'Hybridity', in D. Atkinson, P. Jackson, D. Sibley, and N. Washbourne (eds.), *Cultural Geography: A Critical Dictionary of Key Concepts*, I.B. Taurus, London, pp. 188-193.

Mitchell, T. (1988), *Colonizing Egypt*, Cambridge University Press, Cambridge.

Mitullah, W. (2010), 'Informal Workers in Kenya and Transnational Organizing: the Challenge of Sustainability', in I. Lindell (ed.), *Africa's Informal Workers: Collective Agency, Alliances, and Transnational Organizing*, Nordic Africa Institute, Uppsala, pp. 237-260.

Mooya, M., and C. Cloete (2007), 'Informal Urban Property Markets and Poverty Alleviation: a Conceptual Framework', *Urban Studies*, vol. 44, pp. 147-165.

Murray, M. (2008a), *Taming the Disorderly City: The Spatial Landscape of Johannesburg after Apartheid*, Cornell University Press, Ithaca.

Murray, M. (2008b), 'The City in Fragments: Kaleidoscopic Johannesburg after Apartheid', in *The Spaces of the Modern City: Imaginaries, Politics, and Everyday Life*, G. Prakash and K. Kruse (eds.), Princeton University Press, Princeton, pp. 144-178.

Myers, G. (2008a), 'Sustainable Development and Environmental Justice in African Cities', *Geography Compass*, vol. 2, no. 3, pp. 695-708.

Myers, G. (2008b), 'Peri-Urban Land Reform, Political-Economic Reform, and Urban Political Ecology in Zanzibar', *Urban Geography*, vol. 29, no. 3, pp. 264-288.

Myers, G. (2003), *Verandahs of Power: Colonialism and Space in Urban Africa*, Syracuse University Press, Syracuse, NY.

Myers, G. (2010), 'Social Construction of Peri-Urban Places and Alternative Planning in Zanzibar', *African Affairs (forthcoming)*

Nava, M. (2007), *Visceral Cosmopolitanism: Gender, Culture and the Normalisation of Difference*, Berg, Oxford.

Ngaboh-Smart, F. (2000), '*Secrets* and a New Civic Consciousness', *Research in African Literatures*, vol. 31, no. 1, pp. 129-136.

Ngaboh-Smart, F. (2001), 'Nationalism and the Aporia of National Identity in Farah's *Maps*', *Research in African Literatures*, vol. 32, no. 3, pp. 86-102.

Ngaboh-Smart, F. (2004), *Beyond Empire and Nation: Postnational Arguments in the Fiction of Nuruddin Farah*, Rodopi, Amsterdam

Ngugi wa Thiong'o (1986), *Decolonising the Mind: the Politics of Language in African Literature*, James Currey, London.

Njoh, A. (2003), *Planning in Contemporary Africa: The State, Town Planning and Society in Cameroon*, Ashgate, Aldershot.

Nunan, F. and N. Devas (2004), 'Accessing Land and Services: Exclusion or Entitlement?', in N. Devas (ed.), *Urban Governance, Voice, and Poverty in the Developing World*, Earthscan, London, pp. 164-185.

Nussbaum, M. and A. Sen (1993), 'Introduction', in M. Nussbaum and A. Sen (eds.), *The Quality of Life*, Clarendon Press, Oxford, pp. 1-6.

Nuttall, S. (2008), 'Literary City', in S. Nuttall and A. Mbembe (eds.), *Johannesburg: The Elusive Metropolis,* Duke University Press, Durham, NC, pp. 195-218.

Omasombo, J. (2005), 'Kisangani: a City at its Lowest Ebb', in A. Simone and A. Abouhani (eds.), Urban Africa: Changing Contours of Survival in the City, Codesria Books, Dakar, pp. 96-119.

Payne, G. (2002), *Land, Rights, and Innovation: Improving Tenure Security for the Urban Poor,*ITDG Publishing. London.

Pieterse, E. (2008a), *City Futures: Confronting the Crisis of Urban Development*, Zed Books, London.

Pieterse, E. (2008b), 'Towards an Agenda for Action on African Urbanization: An Argument Arising from the African Urban Innovations Workshop', African Center for Cities, Cape Town.

Portes, A. (1997), 'Globalization from Below: The Rise of Transnational Communities', paper from the ESRC Transnational Communities Program (available online at http://www.transcomm.ox.ac.uk).

Potts, D. (2009). 'The Slowing of Sub-Saharan Africa's Urbanization: Evidence and Implications for Urban Livelihoods', *Environment and Urbanization*, vol. 21, no. 1, pp. 253-259.

Potts, D. (2011), *Circular Migration in Sub-Saharan Africa: Re-inventing the Wheel?* James Currey, Woodbridge, UK.

Prestholdt, J. (2008), *Domesticating the World: African Consumerism and the Genealogies of Globalization*, University of California Press, Berkeley.

Rawls, J. (1971), *A Theory of Justice*, Harvard University Press, Cambridge, MA.

Robins, S. (2006), 'When Shacks Ain't Chic! Planning for "Difference" in Post-Apartheid Cape Town', in S. Bekker and A. Leilde (eds.), *Reflections on Identity in Four African Cities*, African Minds, Johannesburg, pp. 97-117.

Robinson, J. (2006), *Ordinary Cities: Between Modernity and Development*, Routledge, Abdingdon, UK.

Robinson, J. (1998), '(Im)mobilizing Space - Dreaming of Change', in H. Judin and I. Vladislavic (eds.), *Blank: Architecture, Apartheid and After*, NAi Publishers, Rotterdam, pp. 163-171.

Robinson, J. (1990), '"A Perfect System of Control"? State Power and "Native Locations" in South Africa', *Environment and Planning D: Society and Space*, vol. 8, no. 2, pp. 135-162.

Roy, A. (2005). 'Urban Informality: toward an Epistemology of Planning', *Journal of the American Planning Association*, vol. 71, no. 2, pp. 147-158.

Schler, L. (2007), 'The Unwritten History of Ethnic Co-existence in Colonial Africa: an Example from Douala, Cameroon', in P. Ahluwalia, L. Bethlehem, and R. Ginio (eds.), Violence and Non-Violence in Africa, Routledge, London, pp. 27-43.

Sen, A. (1993), 'Capability and Well-Being', in M. Nussbaum and A. Sen (eds.), *The Quality of Life*, Clarendon Press, Oxford, pp. 30-53.

Sen, A. (1999), *Development as Freedom*, Alfred P. Knopf, New York.

Sheffer, G. (1986), 'A New Field of Study: Modern Diasporas in International Politics', in G. Sheffer (ed.), *Modern Diasporas in International Politics*, Croom Helm, London, pp. 1-15.

Shepherd, N., and N. Murray (2007), 'Introduction: Space, Memory and Identity in the Post-Apartheid City, in N. Murray, N. Shepherd, and M. Hall (eds.), *Desire Lines: Space, Memory and Identity in the Post-Apartheid City*, Routledge, London, pp. 1-18.

Sheriff, A. (1987), *Slaves, Spices and Ivory: Integration of an East African Commercial Empire into the World Economy, 1770-1873*, James Currey, London.

Simatele, D., and T. Binns (2008), 'Motivation and Marginalization in African Urban Agriculture: the Case of Lusaka, Zambia', *Urban Forum*, vol. 19, pp. 1-21.

Simone, A. (2010), *City Life from Jakarta to Dakar*, Routledge, London.

Simone, A. (2007), 'Assembling Douala: Imagining Forms of Urban Sociality. In *Urban imaginaries: locating the modern city*, Alev Cinar and Thomas Bender, eds. (Minneapolis: University of Minnesota Press), pp. 79-99.

Simone, A. (2006), 'Pirate Towns: Reworking Social and Symbolic Infrastructures in Johannesburg and Douala', *Urban Studies*, vol. 43, no. 2, pp. 357-370.

Simone, A. (2004), *For the City Yet to Come*, Duke University Press, Durham, NC.

Soja, E. (2000), *Postmetropolis: Critical Studies of Cities and Regions*, Blackwell, Oxford.

Trefon, T. (2009). 'Hinges and Fringes: Conceptualizing the Peri-Urban in Central Africa', in F. Locatelli and P. Nugent (eds.), *African Cities: Competing Claims on Urban Spaces*, Brill, Leiden.

UN Habitat (2008), *State of African Cities Report*, UN Habitat, Nairobi.

Varley, A. (2002), 'Private or Public: Debating the Meaning of Tenure Legalization', *International Journal of Urban and Regional Research*, vol. 26, pp. 449-461.

Waste Management Unit, Lusaka City Council (2006), 'Waste Collection Services in Peri-Urban Areas', unpublished report, Lusaka City Council Waste Management Unit, Lusaka.

Watson, V. (2007), 'Engaging with Difference: Understanding the Limits of Multiculturalism in Planning in the South African Context', in N. Murray, N. Shepherd, and M.Hall (eds.), *Desire Lines: Space, Memory and Identity in the Post-Apartheid City*, Routledge, London, pp. 67-79.

Williams, R. J. (2006), '"Doing History": Nuruddin Farah's *Sweet and Sour Milk*, Subaltern Studies, and the Postcolonial Trajectory of Silence', *Research in African Literatures*, vol. 37, no. 4, pp. 161-176.

Wright, G. (1991), *The Politics of Design in French Colonial Urbanism*, University of Chicago Press, Chicago.

Yeoh, B. (2001), 'Postcolonial cities', *Progress in Human Geography*, vol. 25, no. 3, pp. 456-468.

Zeleza, P. T. (2005), 'The Politics and Poetics of Exile: Edward Said in Africa', *Research in African Literatures*, vol. 36, no. 3, pp. 1-22.

ABOUT THE AUTHOR

Garth Andrew Myers is Professor of Geography and African/African American Studies at the University of Kansas. Professor Myers' teaching and research focuses on urban development, environmental issues, and cultural geography in Africa. His publications include *Verandahs of Power: Colonialism and Space in Urban Africa, Disposable Cities: Garbage, Governance and Sustainable Development in Urban Africa,* and *Cities in Contemporary Africa.* He holds a BA from Bowdoin College, an MA in African Area Studies and a PhD in Geography from UCLA.

www.ingramcontent.com/pod-product-compliance
Lightning Source LLC
Chambersburg PA
CBHW080210300326
41934CB00039B/3447

The growth of cities is one of the most significant aspects of the contemporary transformation of African societies. Cities in Africa are the sites of major political, economic and social innovation, and thus play a critical role in national politics, domestic economic growth and social development. They are also key platforms for interaction with the wider world and mediate between global and national contexts. Cities are variously positioned in global flows of resources, goods and ideas, and are shaped by varied historical trajectories and local cultures. The result is a great diversity of urban societies across the continent. Cities in Africa are not only growing rapidly but are also undergoing deep political, economic and social transformation. They are changing in ways that defy usual notions of urbanism. In their dazzling complexity, they challenge most theories of the urban. African cities represent major challenges as well as opportunities. Both need to be understood and addressed if a sustainable urban future is to be achieved on the continent.

   The Urban Cluster of the Nordic Africa Institute, through its research, seeks to contribute to an understanding of processes of urban change in Africa. This discussion paper by Professor Garth Myers, commissioned by the Urban Cluster, is a valuable contribution to shaping the research agenda on urban Africa.

GARTH ANDREW MYERS is Professor of Geography and African/African American Studies at the University of Kansas. Professor Myers' teaching and research focuses on urban development, environmental issues, and cultural geography in Africa. His publications include *Verandahs of Power: Colonialism and Space in Urban Africa*, *Disposable Cities: Garbage, Governance and Sustainable Development in Urban Africa*, and *Cities in Contemporary Africa*. He holds a BA from Bowdoin College, an MA in African Area Studies and a PhD in Geography from UCLA.

Nordiska ❧ Afrikainstitutet
The Nordic Africa Institute

Nordiska Afrikainstitutet
(The Nordic Africa Institute)
P.O. Box 1703
SE- 751 47 Uppsala, Sweden
www.nai.uu.se

ISBN 978-91-7106-677-0
90000

9 789171 066770

DISCUSSION paper 62

Ethnicity and Democratisation in Africa

CHALLENGES FOR POLITICS AND DEVELOPMENT

OSITA A. AGBU

Nordiska Afrikainstitutet
The Nordic Africa Institute